# NOW, WHO WOULD HAVE SAID THAT?

# NOW, WHO WOULD HAVE SAID THAT?

H E Richardson

ATHENA PRESS
LONDON

First Published 2006 by
ATHENA PRESS
Queen's House, 2 Holly Road
Twickenham TW1 4EG
United Kingdom

Printed for Athena Press

# A BRIEF LAUGH AT LIFE

I dedicate this book to four-year-old Lydia Croft, who had to have both her legs amputated after contracting meningitis. Just to see this adorable young girl smiling happily and riding her bicycle with her artificial limbs as if she never had a care in the world is absolutely inspirational.

# CONTENTS

# NOW, WHO WOULD HAVE SAID THAT?

I would like to start with a true incident that happened around two years ago. We were on a coach trip through France, just passing Dunkirk when the driver told us to look out of the left hand side windows, as we would shortly be passing a cemetery. He told us it was the resting place of the man who invented crosswords. It seemed to be true, as the headstones were all black and the pathways around them all white. The driver added that if we were ever in the area again and wished to visit the man's grave, we would find it six rows down, five across.

# PARTY POLITICS

'I have climbed to the top of the greasy pole.'

*Benjamin Disraeli, on being elected Prime Minister*

'Fear in politics often ends in folly.'

*Anon*

'Not a chip off the old block, but the old block itself.'

*Edmund Burke referring to William Pitt the elder*

'The House of Commons is the longest running farce in the West End.'

*Sir Cyril Smith*

'The distance is nothing; it's only the first step that is difficult.'

*Marquise de Deffand*

'A parliament can do anything except make a man a woman, and a woman a man.'

*Henry Herbert, Second Earl of Pembroke*

'The happiness of society is the end of government.'

*John Adams*

'Politics is war without bloodshed, while war is politics with bloodshed.'

*Mao Tse-tung, 1938 lecture*

'If we are attacked we can only defend ourselves with guns not with butter.'

*Joseph Goebbels, Berlin speech, 1936*

'Would you rather have butter or guns? Preparedness makes us powerful. Butter merely makes us fat.'

*Hermann Goering, Hamburg speech, 1936*

'I want to be the white man's brother, not his brother-in-law.'

*Martin Luther King, New York speech, 1962*

'The great nations have always acted like gangsters and the small nations like prostitutes.'

*Stanley Kubrick, The Guardian, 5 June 1963*

'A man who can't ride two bloody horses at once has no right to a job in the bloody circus.'

*James Maxton, Labour debate, 1932*

'I was determined that I would not let the Government be brought down by a couple of tarts.'

*Sir Harold Macmillan, speaking about the Profumo Affair*

'The only safe pleasure for a parliamentarian is a bag of boiled sweets.'

*Julian Critchley, Listener, June 1982*

'The most successful politicians are those that are most economic with the truth.'

*Anon*

'The Germans… are going to be squeezed, as a lemon is squeezed – until the pips squeak.'

*Sir Eric Geddes, after the end of World War I, 1919*

'We are in an armed conflict; that is the phrase I have used. There has been no declaration of war.'

*Sir Anthony Eden, speaking of the Suez crisis.*

'If you want anything said, ask a man. If you want something done, ask a woman.'

*Margaret Thatcher*

'Be nice to people on your way up because you'll meet them on your way down.'

*Margaret Thatcher*

# SIR WINSTON CHURCHILL

During a row in the House of Commons, *Lady Nancy Astor* told *Churchill*: 'If you were my husband, I'd put poison in your coffee.' To which he replied, 'If you were my wife, I'd drink it.'

On another occasion in parliament, a woman member pointed out to *Churchill* that his flies were open, to which he replied, 'No need to panic, madam, dead birds do not fall out of their nests.'

It is said that *Churchill* was interviewing a man for a gardening job at Chartwell and he asked the man about his family. The man replied, 'I have a wife and sixteen children who I love dearly.' To which *Churchill* is said to have replied, 'I love my cigar dearly, but I do take it out of my mouth now and again.'

The author, *George Bernard Shaw* once sent two first night tickets to one of his plays to *Sir Winston Churchill* with a note saying: 'Bring a friend if you have one.' *Churchill* replied, 'I'd like to have a ticket for a second performance if there is one.'

# WAR AND PEACE

*Josef Stalin*, when asked to conciliate with the pope, said, 'How many divisions has he got?'

'The quickest way of ending a war is to loose it.'

George Orwell, *Polemic, May 1946*

'I gave my life for freedom – this I know for those who bade me fight had told me so.'

*William Norman Ewar, 1917*

'Greater love than this, he said, no man has that he lay down his wife for his friend.'

*James Joyce, Ulysses*

'I don't mind you being killed but I object to your being taken prisoner.'

*Lord Kitchener, spoken to the Prince of Wales during the First World War*

'When you go home, tell them of us and say, "For your tomorrow, we gave our today".'

*John Maxwell Edmonds, suggested war memorial inscription*

'It became necessary to destroy the town in order to save it.'

*US army report on Ben Tre, Vietnam, 8 February 1968*

'Victory has a hundred fathers, but defeat is an orphan.'

*Curtis E Lemay, diary entry, 1946*

'War is too serious a matter to be entrust to military men.'

*Georges Clemenceau*

'I have Scinde.'

*Sir Charles Napier, a report sent to Hydrabad after winning the Battle of Scinde (India), 1843*

# KINGS AND QUEENS

'He speaks to me as if I were a public meeting.'

*Queen Victoria, referring to Gladstone*

'I know I have the body of a weak and feeble woman, but I have the heart and stomach of a king and a king of England too.'

*Elizabeth I, in a speech at Tilbury to her troops on the eve of the Armada*

Although happy in his marriage to Catherine of Braganza and the couple would survive his numerous affairs, *Charles II* had two great passions in life: the first his love of ladies and then the love of horses. He therefore not only had a stable of horses, he also had what could only be described as a stable of mistresses.

One afternoon, one of the better known mistresses, Nell Gwyn, was crossing Whitehall when she saw coming towards her another mistress, the Duchess of Portsmouth. The Duchess spoke, 'Why, Nell, you look dressed enough, as fit to be a queen.'

Nell replied, 'Yes, true and whore enough to be a Duchess.'

*King Michael of Romania*, on being dethroned in 1921, was heard to say, 'It is hard for a king to find a job.'

*Edward VII* was another who had a string of mistresses, including the actress, Lily Langtree, but at a time when this was acceptable. At the end of his life, when he was lying ill in Windsor Castle, the following message was received along the electric wire: 'He is not better, he is much the same.'

*George V* was another monarch who was not popular with his subjects, so much so that when the Great War broke out against Germany in 1914 he had to change the family name from Saxe Coburg Gotha to Windsor.

When he lay dying, one of his doctors remarked, 'Sire, when you are feeling better we will make the arrangements for you to spend time in Bognor Regis.'

The King is said to have replied, 'Bugger Bognor.'

*King Farouk of Egypt*, when deposed in 1952, remarked: 'Soon there will only be five kings left – the King of England, the King of Hearts, the King of Diamonds, the King of Clubs and the King of Spades.'

'For seventeen years he did nothing at all but kill animals and stick stamps.'

*Sir Harold Nicolson in reference to the life of King George V*

'It is the gold filling in the mouth of decay.'

*John Osborne on royalty*

*Prince Charles and Princess Diana* were preparing for their honeymoon aboard the Royal Yacht *Britannia* and the valet asked the prince if there was anything he particularly wanted packed, to which the prince replied, 'Don't forget my fishing rods.'

*Andrew Morton, Diana*

QUEEN *ELIZABETH* II

'In the words of one of my more sympathetic correspondents, it has turned out to be an *Annus Horriblis*.'

*Elizabeth II, 1992*

# PAST PRESIDENTS

'There can be no whitewash at the Whitehouse.'

*Richard Nixon, New York Times, 1 May 1973*

'People have got to know whether or not their president is a crook. Well, I'm not a crook.'

*Richard Nixon, New York Times, 18 November 1973*

'I brought myself down. I gave them a sword and they stuck it in…'

*Richard Nixon in a TV interview, May 1977*

'Remember, I am a Ford, not a Lincoln.'

*Gerald Ford, taking the oath for vice President, 1973*

'The government big enough to give you everything you want is big enough to take away everything you have.'

*Gerald Ford, speech in New York*

'It was involuntary. They sank my boat.'

*John F Kennedy, on being asked how he became a war hero, 1965*

'People who like this sort of thing will find this the sort of thing they like.'

*Abraham Lincoln, discussing a book*

# SONG AND DANCE

'Give me your laundry list and I will write you a song.'

Gaiocomo Rossini

'The opera ain't over till the fat lady sings.'

Dan Cook

'It's like playing a fruit machine – if you pull all the right leavers you hit the jackpot.'

Irving Berlin, when asked how he wrote a hit song

'There are two golden rules for an orchestra: start together and finish together. The public doesn't give a damn what goes on in between.'

Sir Thomas Beecham

'Opera is when a guy gets stabbed in the back and instead of bleeding, he sings.'

Ed Gardner

'Madam, you have between your legs and instrument capable of giving pleasure to thousands and all you can do is scratch it.'

Sir Thomas Beecham to a cellist

The composer Irving Berlin had an altercation one afternoon with the comedian Phil Silvers (Sergeant Bilco), who had said to him that he should ring up Fort Knox and ask how they were looking after all the money he was earning. That evening at home, Berlin told his wife about the incident, saying, 'I never found that man amusing. To me he is about as funny as a custard pie at a funeral.'

# STAGE AND SCREEN

'I'll cry all the way to the bank.'

Liberace on being informed that the critics had<br>savaged his latest show

'I never forget a face, but in your case I'll be glad to make an exception.'

Groucho Marx

*Billy Wilder*: 'I remember you! Weren't you big in films once?'

*Norma Desmond*: 'Yes, but the films got smaller.'

'Don't Clap too hard – it's a very old building.'

John Osborne, The Entertainer

'Will the people in the cheaper seats just clap your hands? And the rest of you, if you'll just rattle your jewellery.'

John Lennon The Royal Variety Show, 1963

'A verbal contract isn't worth the paper it's written on.'

Sam Goldwyn

'A trip through a sewer in a glass-bottomed boat.'

*Wilson Mizner, referring to Hollywood*

'Money can't buy friends, but you get a better class of enemy.'

*Spike Milligan*

'Remember, you're fighting for this woman's honour which is probably more then she ever did.'

*Bert Kalmar, 'Duck Soup' spoken by Groucho Marx*

*George Bernard Shaw* was having dinner with an American actress when she said to him, 'Imagine that if you and I were to get married with my looks and your intelligence think what wonderful children we could have.' To which Shaw replied, 'Have you thought about them having my looks and your brains? Surely that would be a disaster.'

The comedian, *Bernard Manning*, owns a night club in Manchester where he employs his mother as the receptionist. When asked why he employed her there, he replied, 'Well if she's going to take money from the till it will still be in the family.'

*Brian Rix* was performing one of his farces at the Whitehall Theatre and when he came off stage he noticed the comedian *Terry Thomas* had been watching him. He asked Terry, 'What sort of time do you think the show will run for?' Terry Thomas looked at his watch and said, 'What time is it now?'

'She ran the whole gamut of emotions from a to b.'

*Dorothy Parker in reference to Katherine Hepburn*
*in a Broadway show.*

Why do today what you can put off until tomorrow?

*Harold Pinter*

'All I need to make a comedy is a park, a policeman and a pretty girl.'

*Charlie Chaplin, 1964*

'Being a star has made it possible for me to get insulted in places where the average Negro could never hope to get insulted.'

*Sammy Davis Junior*

*Graham Walton*, the father of the Walton girl sextuplets, said: 'Now my girls are eighteen the boys are coming to the house to meet my delightful daughters. It felt like giving a Stradivarius Violin to a gorilla.

When asked his opinion of the actress *Barbara Stanwyck*, *Walter Matthau* replied, 'When she is good she is good, but when she is bad she is brilliant.'

# BARE-FACED FACTS

'She just wore enough for modesty, no more.'

Robert Buchanhan

*Joan Rivers* and *Beryl Reid* were in conversation on a television show and *Joan Rivers* told her that another elderly woman made a gobbling sound when she had sex, to which *Beryl Reid* replied, 'Don't we all?'

'The next act tonight should have been the Russian Michaelov and his performing bear, but after seeing the act the manager made him put his clothes on.'

Theatre compère at the Windmill Theatre

# MAE WEST

'It's not the men in my life that count, it's the life in my men – I'm no angel.'

*Mae West*

'I always say, keep a diary and some day it'll keep me.'

*Every Day's a Holiday, 1937*

'Goodness what beautiful diamonds.'
'Goodness had nothing to do with it.'

*Night after Night, 1932*


'Let's get out of these wet clothes and into a dry martini.'

*Every Day's a Holiday, 1937*

# OSCAR WILDE

'A cynic is a man who knows the price of every-thing and the value of nothing.'

*Oscar Wilde, Lady Windermere's Fan*

'The truth is rarely pure and never simple.'

*The Importance of Being Earnest*

'I have nothing to declare except my genius.'

*On being stopped by customs officers*
*in New York Harbour*

'I can resist anything except temptation.'

*Lady Windermere's Fan*

'We are all in the gutter, but some of us are looking
at the stars.'

*Lady Windermere's Fan*

'Experience is the name everyone gives to their
mistakes.'

*Lady Windermere's Fan*

'The English country gentlemen galloping after the
fox – the unspeakable in full pursuit of the uneat-
able.'

*A Woman of No Importance*

'Work is the curse of the drinking classes.'

*Oscar Wilde*

'[He] hasn't an enemy in the world, and none of
his friends like him.'

*Oscar Wilde, on Bernard Shaw*

'There is only one thing worse in the world then
being talked about, and that is not being talked
about.'

*The Picture of Dorian Gray*

'A man cannot be too careful in the choice of his enemies.'

*The Picture of Dorian Gray*

'Ah, well, then I suppose I shall have to die beyond my means.'

*On being told to expect a large fee for his surgery*

'One should never trust a woman who tells one her real age. A woman who would tell one that, would tell one anything.'

*Oscar Wilde*

'Please don't shoot the pianist. He is doing his best.'

*Oscar Wilde*

# CHILDREN'S CORNER

A child tells his mother that he has been told to take some money to school to pay for sixty-five roses. As it seems to be a strange request the mother decides to go to the school. When she explains her son's remarks, the teacher explains it was for cystic fibrosis.

*Told by Eamon Andrews*

A teacher asked her class: 'We all know that the female swan is called the pen; can any of you tell me what a male swan is called?'

A small boy stood up saying, 'I know, Miss, it's called a pencil.'

A Sunday school teacher asked her class, 'Do any of you know where God lives?'

A girl stood up to say, 'He lives in our bathroom.'

'Why do you say that?' said the teacher.

'Well,' replied the girl, 'every morning my Dad knocks on the door and shouts: "God, are you still in there?"'

A small boy was about to leave his friend's birthday party and asked his friend's father why he had not shown him his trick.

'What trick is that?' asked the father.

'My mum and dad tell me you can drink like a fish,' replied the boy.

A woman was asking her neighbours' son about the new cat they had.

'So, what do you call him?' she asked.

'We call him a kitten,' he replied.

Some friends of mine with a ten-year-old son were having some problems with his behaviour, so his father told him that when he went to bed that night he should say his prayers and ask Jesus to make him a better boy. The boy promised that he would. Sitting at breakfast the following morning, the father asked, 'Did you talk to Jesus last night in bed?'

'Yes, I did Dad.'

'And what did Jesus say?'

'He told me not to worry as he was the same as me at my age.'

A small boy on his first visit to church had been given a shilling to put in the collection plate. When his mother asked him if he had liked the service he replied, 'Yes, Mum, all that singing; it was well worth a shilling.'

# LOVE AND MARRIAGE

'One fool at least in every married couple.'

*Henry Fielding*

'It's all any reasonable child can expect if the dad is present at the conception.'

*Joe Orton, Entertaining Mr Sloane*

'Marriage is not a word, it is a sentence.'

*King Vidor, The Crowd, 1928*

'Doris Greenfield left her husband because she was afraid of him. She decided six months later to return to him for the same reason.'

*Iris Murdoch, The Bell 1958*

'Love is the delusion that one women differs from another.'

*HL Mencken, Chrestomathy, 1949*

'Continental people have a sex life; the English have hot water bottles.'

*George Mikes, How to be an Alien, 1946*

'Love is a disease for which there is no cure.'

*George Eliot*

'Never marry a man who hates his mother, because he'll end up hating you.'

*Jacqueline Kennedy Onassis*

'It doesn't matter what you do in the bedroom as long as you don't do it in the street and frighten the horses.'

*Mrs Patrick Campbell*

'A women can become a man's friend only in the following stages – first as an acquaintance, next as a mistress, and only then as a friend.'

*Anton Chekov, Uncle Vanya*

'Medicine is my lawful wife, literature is my mistress; when I get tired of one, I spend the night with the other.'

*Anton Chekov*

'Bloody men are like bloody buses – you wait for about a year and as soon as one approaches your stop, two or three others appear.'

*Wendy Cope, Bloody Men, 1992*

'Love is like the measles; we all have to go through it.'

*Jerome K Jerome*

'Do you think your mother and I should have lived comfortably together if ever we had been married?'

*John Gay, The Beggar's Opera*

'For marriage is like life in this – that it is a field of battle, and not a bed of roses.'

*Robert Louis Stevenson*

'Being a husband is a full-time job, that is why so many husbands fail they cannot give it their full attention.'

*Anon*

'In the midst of life we are in debt.'

*Ethel Watts Mumford*

'There is nothing worse for a women then being all dressed up and having nowhere to go.'

*Anon*

'He told me it was artificial respiration but now I find I'm to have his child.'

*Anthony Burgess, Inside Mr Enderby*

'Familiarity breeds contempt – and children.'

*Mark Twain*

'Once a woman has given you her heart, you can never get rid of the rest of her.'

*Sir John Vanbrugh, The Relapse*

'The proper union of gin and vermouth is a great and sudden glory; it is one of the happiest marriages on earth, and one of the shortest lived.'

*Bernard De Voto*

'The more I see of men, the more I admire dogs.'

*Jean-Marie Roland*

# SPORTING LIFE

'Honey, I just forgot to duck.'

*Jack Dempsey, said to his wife after losing his
World Heavyweight title in September 1926*

'The bigger they are, the further they have to fall.'

*Robert (Bob) Fitzsimmons prior to a championship
boxing match in 1900*

'Boxing is just show business with blood.'

*Frank Bruno, December 1991*

'Some people think football is a matter of life and
death… I can assure them it is much more serious
than that.'

*Bill Shankley, October 1981*

'I spent a lot of money on booze, birds and fast cars
– the rest I just squandered.'

*George Best*

# DEFINITIONS

What has a moo at one end and milk at the other?
A cow.

Anon

What has a lot of noise coming from one end and no responsibility from the other?
A baby.

Anon

'A triumph of the embalmer's art.'

Gore Vidal in reference to Ronald Reagan

What's the definition of a mistress?
It is a miss found between a mister and a mattress.

Anon

'A monstrous carbuncle on the face of a much-loved and elegant friend.'

Prince Charles in reference to the extensions at the Tate Gallery

# MISCELLANEOUS

*John Milton*, when talking to a friend, suggested that the man should have his daughter taught another language to which his friend replied: 'One tongue is enough for any woman.'

'There was things which he stretched, but mainly he told the truth.'

*Mark Twain, Huckleberry Finn*

'You can build a throne of bayonets, but you cannot sit on it.'

*W B Singe*

'My only qualification for being put at the head of the navy, is that I [feel] very much at sea.'

*Edward Carson, Life of Lord Carson*

'Money is like muck, not good unless spread.'

*Francis Bacon, Essays XV, 1625*

Notice in doctors' surgery: 'If you cannot speak or read English please bring a translator with you.'

Notice in jeweller's window: 'Have your ears pierced while you wait.'

'Life is just one damned thing after another.'

Elbert Hubbard

'Life is a gamble, at terrible odds – if it was a bet you wouldn't take it.'

Tom Stoppard

'Men will confess to treason, murder, arson, false teeth. or a wig. How many of them will own up to a lack of humour?'

Frank Moore Colby

'Moral indignation is jealousy with a halo.'

H G Wells

'When you don't have money the problem is food, when you do have money it's sex.'

J P Donlevy

'It serves me right for putting all my eggs in one bastard.'

Dorothy Parker

'Nobody loves a fairy when she's forty.'

Arthur Le Clerq, 1934

'As he rose like the rocket, he would fall like a stick.'

Thomas Paine in reference to Edmund Burke losing a political<br>debate

'Most people posture New York as an attractive, cosmopolitan city; whereas in reality it is little more than a rat-infested rubbish tip. The rats out-number the residents by more than ten to one.'

Naiomi Klein

An American boxer being interviewed recently said: 'I have fought in more then twenty contests in the last six months.'

The reporter replied, 'God, what state were you in after that?'

The boxer replied, 'I was in Texas.'

*Boswell*: 'Is not the Giant's Causeway worth seeing?'

*Samuel Johnson*: 'Yes, it was worth seeing, but not worth going to see.'

The Life of Samuel Johnson

'I could come back to America to die – but never, never to live.'

Henry James in a letter to his mother

'A sharp tongue is the only edged tool that grows keener with constant use.'

Washington Irvine, The Sketch Book, 1820

'Truth exists – only lies are invented.'

George Braque

'Whatever women do they must do twice as well as men to be thought half as good. Luckily, this is not difficult.'

Charlotte Whitton

'I have lost friends, some through death and some through failing to cross the street.'

*Virginia Woolf*

'In order to establish a lie one must first eradicate the truth.'

*Virginia Woolf*

The man who makes no mistakes does not usually make anything.

*Edward Phelps*

What is now proved was once only imagined.

*William Blake*

To err is human, but to really foul things up requires a computer.

*Farmers' Almanac, 1978*

Advice is seldom welcome; and those who want it the most, always like it the least.

*Lord Chesterfield*

I wish my deadly foe no worse, than want of friends, and empty purse.

*William Shakespeare*

And if the blind lead the blind, both shall fall into the ditch.

*The Bible, KJV, Matthew 15:14*

The happiest women, like the happiest nations, have no history.

*George Elliot, The Mill On The Floss*

Asked why he had opened his dry cleaner's shop next to a church, the man replied, 'I feel that cleanliness should always come next to Godliness.'

*Alistair Cooke, Letters From America*

''Tis strange what a man may do, and a woman yet think him an angel.'

*William Makepeace Thackeray*

'When you have nothing to say, say nothing.'

*William Makepeace Thackeray*

Putin meets Cretin

*Protest banner at meeting between President Bush
and the Russian leader*

If you can see the light at the end of the tunnel it is probably a train coming towards you.

*Paul Dickson, Washington Union, November 1978*

Life is just a sexually transmitted disease.

*Graffiti on the London Underground*

I am a Marxist of the Groucho variety.

*Graffiti on the Paris Metro*

Beat the eggs well the way you would like to beat the next-door neighbour's children.

*The Sally Jessie Rafael Show*

If it moves, salute it: if it doesn't, pick it up: if you can't pick it up, paint it.

*Army rules and regulations*

'He was bold man who first ate an oyster.'

*Jonathan Swift*

'The cook was a good cook as good cooks go and as good cooks go, she went.'

*H H Munro (Saki), 'Reginald on Besetting Sins', Reginald*

'Life is too short to stuff a mushroom.'

*Shirley Conran*

'Kissing don't last: cookery do!'

*George Meredith*

# ANONYMOUS

There is an old Arabic saying that aptly fits the current situation in Iraq. It goes: If you come home and your house is on fire, be sure that the fire is out before you start to redecorate it.

Never give a male friend money if he threatens to kill himself; give him a gun.

HER

What's the point of owning a bike if you don't know how to ride it?

HER

If this place is haunted by ghosts and ghoulies, I hope I get caught by the ghosts.

Anon

Child: 'Mummy, are Tories born wicked, or do they grow up that way?'

Mother: 'They are born wicked and grow up worse.'

Anon

It's hard for a man with a wig to keep his hair on.

HER

You may have a problem if you have a tendency to speak before you think.

*Anon*

The only way to stand is on, the only way to fall is off.

*Anon*

The women was so dumb that she thought Little Red Riding Hood was a Russian contraceptive.

*Anon*

The town that I was born in was so small that the Lord Mayor and the Village Idiot were the same person.

*Anon*

You would not call this a one-horse town if you had to pick up the manure.

*Anon*

The least favoured guests at the wedding reception are usually sat next to the band.

*Anon*

The quickest way to do things is to do them one thing at a time.

*Anon*

Men seem to spend most of their time looking forward to the past.

*Anon*

If you have to grasp the nettle, be sure to grasp it with care.

*Anon*

The east end of a city is always the worst end, as that is where the wind blows the rubbish.

*HER*

When they changed their name from 'The Silver Beatles' to 'The Beatles', it brought them success, but would they have been so successful if they had called themselves 'The Cockroaches'?

*HER*

If you can attract a women by whistling to her, you will never need to buy a dog.

*HER*

If you can't see further then the end of your nose you must be short sighted.

*HER*

A girl must be careful when she introduces her new boyfriend to her best girlfriend, otherwise her best girlfriend will soon become her worst enemy.

*HER*

If you act like a doormat, someone will always tread on you.

*HER*

A casual relationship needs serious responsibility.

*Anon*

A wife is a young man's mistress, a middle-aged man's companion and an old man's nurse.

*Anon*

There is nothing wrong in loving thy neighbour, provided nobody tells her husband.

*HER*

You can never plan the future by looking into the past.

*Anon*

Misfortune can often be the result of being married to the wrong person.

*Anon*

Often people who start out as the best of friends finish up as the worst of enemies.

*Anon*

# TAILENDERS

Two neighbours talking:

'I am getting the rolls sent round this morning for my daughter's wedding.'

'Do you mean she is having a Rolls Royce?'

'No, I mean the bread rolls from the bakery.'

I understood from my agent that they were sending a car for me, luckily it missed me.'

Anon

Singer to his audience: 'I do get most of my work from abroad, it seems that nobody wants to employ me here.'

During my service in the army (conscripted) I was posted to Egypt. I hated every minute of it, as I couldn't get out of the envelope.

Anon

*Lord Nuffield*, as a William Morris motor mechanic, applied to join the local golf club. His application was rejected without a reason. Some four years later he applied again as Lord Nuffield, Chairman of British Motors, and was accepted with open arms. He later sacked the members of the committee.

'If she can stand it, I can play it.'

*Julius Epstein, Casablanca*

'Forget it Louis, no Civil War picture ever made a nickel.'

*Irving Thalberg's comment to Louis B Meyer about the film Gone With The Wind 1936*

'Like having your own licence to print money.'

*Roy Thomson on the profit of television programmes*

'Death is nature's way of telling you to slow down.'

*Insurance advert*

'It's a funny old world – a man's lucky if he gets out of it alive.'

*WC Fields*

Charm is a way of getting an answer without having to ask the question.

*Anon*

There are two things to aim for in life: first, to get what you want and after that, to enjoy it.

*Anon*

Fools make the best husbands. Most failures in marriage come from men having brains.

*Anon*

My wife and I were chatting to a neighbour who was telling us about her husband's success as an exhibitor in the areas flower show. She made us smile by saying if we looked in the local paper we could see a picture of him holding up his onions.

A friend of mine was going down to Somerset for a few days break and left in the evening to travel through the night. He got as far as Taunton when the car suddenly broke down. It was a lonely spot but he could see a light in the distance and made his way there. It turned out to be a cottage and the farmer offered to put him up for the night. The farmer and his young wife then asked my friend if he was hungry. When he replied that he was the wife gave him a large piece of Cheddar cheese for his supper. The farmer then told him that they only had one bed and so they would have to share, with him on the inside, the wife in the middle and the farmer on the outside as he had to get up early to go and milk the cows.

In the morning, the farmer left the house and the wife said to my friend, 'Right, now that he has gone you can have anything you like.' So he jumped out of bed and got himself another piece of cheese.

'Die, my dear doctor! That is the last thing I shall do!'

*Lord Palmerston*

'Dying is an art, like everything else.'

*Sylvia Plath, 'Lady Lazarus', Ariel, 1965*

'When I am dead, I hope it might be said: "His sins were scarlet, but his books were read".'

*Hilaire Belloc*

*Dorothy Parker*, on being told that *Calvin Coolidge* had died, said, 'How do they know?'

'I am just going outside and may be gone for some time.'

*Captain Lawrence Oates, last entry in Scott's diary, March 1922*

'I never think of the future. It comes soon enough.'

*Albert Einstein*

'Curtsey while you're thinking what to say. It saves time.'

*Lewis Carroll, the Queen of Hearts in*
*Through the Looking-Glass*

'In Italy, for thirty years under the Borgias, they had warfare, terror, murder, bloodshed; they produced Michelangelo, Leonardo Da Vinci and the Renaissance. In Switzerland, they had brotherly love, five hundred years of democracy and peace and what did they produce? The cuckoo clock.'

*Orson Welles, The Third Man*

'My mother used to say, Delia, if S-E-X ever rears it's ugly head, close your eyes before you see the rest of it.'

*Alan Aykbourne, Bedroom Farce*

'When I hear his steps outside my door, I lie down on the bed, close my eyes, open my legs and think of England.'

*Jonathan Gathorne-Hardy, Lady Hillingdon in*
*The Rise and Fall of the British Nanny, 1972*